A BOOK TO ENTERTAIN

TREASURE HUNT

Written and compiled by Sally Raymond
Illustrated by Anne Parsons

Home Time is a series of six books, each designed to give the busy parent bright ideas!
Each chosen item has been tested with children of various ages with much success.
You will find fresh ideas, with clear instructions, to interest and entertain your child
throughout the year, in any weather, using only basic materials or ingredients.

TREASURE HUNT

WELCOME!

Be clueless no longer. This book has arrived to show you how easily treasure hunting games can be made, played and enjoyed...by everyone!

Transform your wet afternoons and square-eyed children. Activate them awake with a game that is easy to create, cheap to supply and perfect entertainment whatever the time or the place.

Pens, paper and a prize is all you need to get started. Preparing your treasure hunt beforehand is the key to success, which is where this book comes into its own. Sally Raymond passes on tips from her many experiences of clue-concocting and trail-devising over the years.

"I haven't a clue what to do."
Then give them a treasure hunt.

Individuals, mixed ages, parties and family gatherings all welcome the exhilarating fun that is perfectly, personally fashioned to suit their needs. You will be delighted how effectively treasure hunting games entertain, educate and exhaust your children.

!tuo dnif dna no daer

FUN FOR EVERYONE

ANYONE at ANYTIME can enjoy treasure trails. On a wet afternoon at Grandma's, a family celebratory gathering, in the garden, in one room or the whole house.

Don't tell the children, but the merits of these games are many. They provide ACTIVE ENTERTAINMENT, INTERACTION and COMMUNICATION practice. They introduce ADVENTURE and CHALLENGES during the trail.

Children can enjoy treasure hunting by themselves or as part of a team. TEAMWORK can develop spontaneously or be encouraged through the clues. SHARING, TAKING TURNS, RECEIVING and GIVING ADVICE are all useful skills for a child to develop. They must be patient at times, or helpful. They can be responsible for a younger child in the team, practise co-operation or

enjoy the liberty of their own PERSONALISED clues.

The joy of treasure trails is their VERSATILITY. Over the next few pages I hope to pass on the pleasure of creating exciting, educational trails. You will be rewarded when you sit back and watch the gallop of giggling hunters!

GETTING STARTED

Rule number one - start simply! Once you and your hunters are hooked on the action and spirit of adventure a treasure hunt provides, progress onwards and outwards to more complicated trails.

The simplest treasure hunting game can be made in a matter of minutes.

- Lay a trail of coloured arrows around, up, over and beyond… leading to the kitchen cupboard or linen chest, anywhere that treasure can hide.

- The trail can have added obstacles:

For the younger child, devise simple challenges.

'Draw a yellow cat.'

For those that can read, the possibilities are endless.

'Complete this puzzle before moving on.'

Trails that include written clues can lead on from place to place around the house, the garden or village hall, and are guaranteed to waken the spirit of adventure. Let's go…

PICTURE CLUES FOR YOUNG CHILDREN

Trails created with PICTORIAL clues are ideal for the younger child. The designs should be simple, and colourful, and always...

> **REMEMBER WHO YOU ARE WRITING THE CLUES FOR**

- If Freddy's favourite teddy bear has a red bow tie, or his cup has a logo on it, concentrate your artistic energies on these before attempting to draw 'the cupboard under the stairs'.

- Put a word or two underneath your picture to encourage reading, and remember not to hide the clues too well (see Instructions to Hunters, p 37).

- Drawing clues on coloured, distinctive paper will help the child identify their clues, which they should be encouraged to collect (perhaps in a bag or pocket). This will help prepare children for more complicated trails later.

- Surprise your hunters with exciting treasure at the end of their trail (see p 36). Also give them some unexpected treats on the way (suitable goodies they can find alongside their clues).

- Pictures can also be used to encourage reading.

Hide the words that match the pictures IN ONE ROOM. With each answer the hunters find another picture. When all the pictures and words have been matched, a prize is awarded.

- Extend your pictorial possibilities, - use magazines.

- Combine pictures together for simple word-puzzle fun:

The trails can be long, or short. Keep the clues simple. And find an unusual place for your treasure to hide that won't be rumbled before time!

PICTURE CLUES FOR OLDER CHILDREN

Pictorial clues are enjoyed by older children too. Trails that include different styles of clue (mixed trails), can feature picture clues alternately with other ones for variety.

CLUES DO NOT HAVE TO BE DIFFICULT TO BE FUN

- Use a group of pictures from magazines or catalogues for a 'Spot the difference' clue:

Spot the odd one out to find your next clue attached to it

- A whole treasure trail can be organised around the pictures in a home shopping catalogue.

First, go through the catalogue and mark a red cross on each of the items in your trail. Note their page number.

Secondly, decide on a route for your trail and hide letters at intervals so that, as they are collected, they spell out the treasure's location.

Additionally, with a different coloured pen, write the next catalogue page number to be consulted beside each letter. This takes hunters along the trail.

Inform your hunters what format the game is to take. Give them the first page number and then, SIT BACK AND RELAX.

FUN FOR THE EARLY READER

Reading for fun is great **STIMULATION** for early readers. Trails that include pictures and words provide **EDUCATIONAL ENTERTAINMENT**.

- A whole trail can be organised around a new word, or used to reinforce instructions such as behind, in front of, or inside.

> **under** the telephone
> **under** the cup

By following a trail, the hunters can either be suddenly surprised by finding treasure, or can be set a last challenge to raise the level of **ANTICIPATION**. Remember though, that excitement often leads to mistakes, so keep the instructions simple.

*SING A SONG TO GRANDPA
to end your trail.
He will tell you where the
treasure hides!*

*DRAW A PICTURE OF
A BROWN CAT.
Go to where this animal
is fed to find your prize.*

- Seven or eight clues is a good length for most hunters, with perhaps a couple of challenges along the way.

*Find three green pencils on your
way to the red Wellington boots
where your next clue hides.*

*Pile 15 bricks on top of the dining table
then look for your clue under
a chair nearby.*

EASY CLUES IN CODE

Early readers enjoy SIMPLE CODES. These aid their spelling, too. Keep the words simple.

Provide the hunters with the code key at the start of play, then send them off on a trail of simple instructions.

Use different codes, numbers or shapes:

```
        A B C D E F G H I J K L
CODE : Z Y X W V U T S R Q P O

        M N O P Q R S T U V W X Y Z
CODE : N M L K J I H G F E D C B A
```

Decode this message to find where your next clue hides.

```
F M W V I     B L F I     Y V W
```

_ _ _ _ _   _ _ _ _   _ _ _

(Answer: under your bed)

```
        A B C D E F G H I J K L M
CODE : G H I J K L M N O P Q R S

        N O P Q R S T U V W X Y Z
CODE : T U V W X Y Z A B C D E F
```

```
Z K R K V N U T K
```

_ _ _ _ _ _ _ _ _

(Answer: TELEPHONE)

```
        A B C D E F G H I J K L M
CODE : 1 2 3 4 5 6 7 8 9 10 11 12 13

        N O P Q R S T U V W X Y Z
CODE : 14 15 16 17 18 19 20 21 22 23 24 25 26
```

```
20 5 12 5 16 8 15 14 5
```

_ _ _ _ _ _ _ _ _

(Answer: TELEPHONE)

```
        A B C D E F G H I J K L M
CODE : ⇨ ✿ ✱ ◯ I ☆ ♥ ✪ ▼ ★ ▢ ● ?

        N O P Q R S T U V W X Y Z
CODE : ▲ ✕ £ ✓ ◆ ✛ % @ ! ◗ $ ☆ ➤
```

```
% I ● I £ ✪ ✕ ▲ I
```

_ _ _ _ _ _ _ _ _

(Answer: TELEPHONE)

MORE CODES TO CRACK

MIRROR WRITING is fun for all ages of hunter. The alphabet below will help you write in it:

Provide a mirror within reach of young hunters rather than allowing them their own polished glass to run around with!

- As the children get more confident with their reading skills, introduce some riddles and puzzles for them to crack. Keep the clue format CLEAR to encourage reading skills. Young hunters will be entertained and enjoyably challenged.

TRAILS can be designed around a book of clues, presented at the start of play. These clues lead the hunters around to different places where single LETTERS have been located.

For large hunts, when clues may be stumbled across by others, use this type of trail. This lessens the likelihood of interference from others spoiling the fun.

- Use your treasure hunt to delve into UNUSUAL PLACES.

tam htab

write backwards to find where your next clue hides

_ _ _ _   _ _ _

fo 6 egap
salta dlrow eht

write backwards to find where your next clue hides

GAMES FOR STEADY READERS

Treasure hunting games for steady readers are great fun. Personalise your clues to suit the abilities of the hunters.

> **CREATE SIMPLE, EXCITING CLUES**

Begin by choosing 8 or so locations for your trail, then list them.

- SHORT WORDS can be used for strange mnemonics.

sad old flabby armadillo

take first letter of each word to find where your next clue hides

picnic so sweet

take last letter of each word to find where your next clue hides

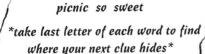

- words with letter REPETITIONS make interesting substitute puzzles.

cucan'c clipperc

change every C for an S to find where your next clue hides

_ _ _ M C _ _ _ I _

change every _ for an A or an R to find where your next clue hides

- LONGER WORDS become a challenge when written backwards.

ENIHCAM GNIHSAW

write backwards to find where your next clue hides

REWARD YRELTUC

write backwards to find where your next clue hides

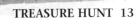

CLEVER CLUES

As children become more confident,
more complicated puzzles can appear
in your trails.

HOT ICE TAPE

first word: its opposite: _ _ _ _

second word: melt it: _ _ _ _ _

third word: remove the E: _ _ _ _

this is where your next clue hides

Peter Piper picked a peck of pickled
_ _ _ _ _ _ _ _ .

*put in the missing word to find
where your next clue hides*

Consider the KNOWLEDGE of
your hunters and write clues
they understand.

• For more than one trail running simultaneously,
use different codes and different coloured paper for clues.
The trails can then overlap without causing confusion.

RHYMES
AND RIDDLES

These must be simple enough for your hunters, but they are good fun to create and bring variety to your trail.

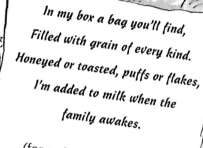

In my box a bag you'll find,
Filled with grain of every kind.
Honeyed or toasted, puffs or flakes,
I'm added to milk when the
family awakes.

(for a clue or prize hidden
in a cereal packet)

When clothes are wet and
need to dry,
Upon the washing line they fly.
The wind blows hard to
aid their flight
But WE are there to hold
them tight.

(leads the hunter to search
among the pegs)

GROUP TREASURE HUNTS

Teams of hunters (4 - 5 per team), make for INTERACTIVE FUN.

Devious manipulation of your players is entirely in your hands. A group of children can be given separate trails to play side-by-side, or one trail to share, to pool their deductive skills.

If there are different abilities within the group, this calls for PERSONALISED clues.

> **CAREFULLY PLAN EACH CLUE WITH YOUR PLAYER IN MIND**

Label each clue for its intended recipient, but to encourage co-operation, suggest that after 30 seconds of uninterrupted

> **REMIND YOUR PLAYERS TO SOLVE EACH CLUE CAREFULLY**

solving, other players are allowed to put in their suggestions, if necessary. Once the clue is solved, the player in charge of that clue can lead the way to find the next.

> **CLUELESS HUNTERS NEED DIRECTION**

> **DIRECT YOUR HUNTERS WITH CLEAR CLUES**

At PARTIES, treasure hunting games can be played competitively between teams. Providing individual treasure for each team will reduce the competitive element. Or you could allow teams to follow the same trail, filling in with other activities for the players awaiting their turn.

TEAM TACTICS FOR
A CLASS, PARTY OR CHILDREN'S FETE

Keep clues DISTINCTIVE for each team. Blue card for one, yellow for another, even though they are hunting along different trails. Bring the teams together at points; make them interact if you like.

(write on blue card)
clue three
STPLY JN JYDDS
(write capitals in black)

(write on yellow card)
clue three
PIK STV LAWH
(write capitals in red)

* this is not your clue. *
*Squeak like mice to attract the team that has your clue.

* this is not your clue. *
Bray like donkeys to attract the team that has your clue.

Listen for a team that are braying like donkeys...they will give you a clue in return for this one.

Listen for a team that are squeaking like mice...they will give you a clue in return for this one.

When you have your correct clue, look at the letters written in red and use your code-breaker to find where your next clue hides.

When you have your correct clue, look at the letters written in black and use your code-breaker to find where your next clue hides.

- Whilst 7 - 8 clues is an average length for an INDIVIDUAL'S trail, longer ones are needed when groups of players are working together, taking turns to answer clues. Allow 2 or 3 clues per player. In my experience...

> **LONG TRAILS GROW TEDIOUS**
> **SHORT TRAILS STUNT STIMULATION**

THEMED HUNTS

Group treasure hunts with a THEME are extra fun. Players can dress in costume, solve clues that are styled to the topic and share out a suitable treasure, fashioned to suit the game.

The conspiratorial thrill of dressing as spies, pirates or mice-after-chocolate-cake, extends the pleasurable value of playing.

You may even find the clues easier to write within the boundaries set by your theme. Remember the ages and interests of your hunters.

The easiest clues to write are the ones whose answers are one or two words long. However, longer answers can usually be dealt with by using missing letters or multiple choice options.

Which treasure is hunted by pirates?
Pieces of six? Pieces of seven?
Pieces of eight?

6 = telephone stand   7 = teapot
8 = double bed

Don't make life difficult by sweating over clues your players then won't understand because the clues are TOO CLEVER.

Here is a trail created around Star Trek. Good treasure is honeycomb nuggets packaged as rock from outer space.

Remember the skills of YOUR players.

CLUE 1:
Be alert! The hairless Trundigs of Warworld eat lasers.
take first letter of each word

_ _ _ _   _ _ _ _ _
(= bath towel)

CLUE 2:
it in numbers telephone has that book a for look
to understand the language of gnelish, read this sentence backwards to find next clue
(= telephone book)

CLUE 3:
The Enterprise traveLs through spacE at warP speed tHirteen to escape frOm cliNgon vEssel.
(put capitals in red)
write down red letters

_ _ _ _ _ _ _ _ _
(= telephone)

CLUE 4:
(PICTURE CLUE)
d + (Spock's ear)   (teddy)

_ _ _ _   _ _ _ _ _
(= dear teddy)

CLUE 5:
Go straight to the s
ick bay.
Dad will give you anti-heslop tablets and your next clue.
(= wherever Dad is)

CLUE 6:
mega big beasties drive back bats before game battle begins
cross out the words that begin with b to find your next clue
(= megadrive game)

ADD THE ACTIVE INGREDIENTS

Additional ACTIVE INGREDIENTS can be added by involving other people in the game, and by incorporating treasure into the game's play. Get the children making treasure beforehand which they can then have the fun of retrieving, or losing, along the trail.

CLUE 1:
Find six pieces of treasure in the bathroom. Buy your next instructions from grandad with this treasure.

CLUE 2:
Make a tower with building bricks. The higher the tower, the more treasure you will receive.

CLUE 3:
Look under a pillow for more treasure and your next instructions.

CLUE 4:
Sing a song to Uncle Jo. If he likes it, he will give you lots of treasure.

CLUE 5:
Find Mum. She has a game for you to play to get more treasure. (game of skittles?)

CLUE 6:
Tidy up the living room floor to find more treasure and your next instructions.

This game is good for GROUP INVOLVEMENT.
All the players take part at every stage.

ADD THE SPICE OF A LITTLE COMPETITION

Planting challenges along the route of team trails allows for an element of COMPETITIVE CHALLENGE.

'Perform a nursery rhyme to Uncle Jo before receiving your next clue.'

'Draw a map for Daddy, showing the way to the park before receiving your next clue.'

This allows an adult to award points to different teams...remembering the skills of their players, keeping their challenges easy and the game lighthearted.

- TIMED CHALLENGES can be similarly used.

Start counting backwards in seconds from a predetermined time when the team begin their challenge. Whatever time is left when they have completed the task, is noted down and rewarded later.

- Challenge the children to a 10-word spelling list. Every word correct scores points for the team.

On completion of the trail, hunters receive bounty weighted according to their scores collected on the way.

COMPETITIVE teams must be fairly matched, or bonuses awarded to those lacking age or experience...use your judgment wisely and keep it FUN.

BRING YOUR TREASURE HUNTS ALIVE!

To really bring treasure hunts alive, plan some surprises along the way.

- Add a clue that calls for a magnifying glass, or a magic pen to uncover instructions…clues that incorporate strange messages, humour or riddles - they're all fun to find and simple to provide.

- Clue-format must always be DISTINCTIVE to help the game run smoothly. For teams, keep clues different in colour and design to prevent confusion; fairy letters versus pirate scrolls, circular messages on scraps of green wallpaper or yellow triangular messages.

- Codes and maps add further adventure, suspense and excitement. Alternatively, write a word in red on each clue's corner. When the trail is complete, the words, when taken in order, spell out the bounty's location. Words or letters can be used, jumbling up the order for older players.

THE EXCITEMENT GROWS

Along the route of the trail you can hide snippets of treasure or tokens exchangeable for bounty later.

- To keep the lid on open warfare, each team can only collect tokens or treasure presented in their team colour, which, like the clues, are not too well hidden.
  (This discourages hunters from wrecking the house in pursuit of their goal!)

Competitive trails are good for parties, mixed ages or for competing individuals...they also allow you some scope for including additional educational elements suitable for your particular players.

Incorporate school's table-learning homework or pamper to an individual's skill. Keep challenges short and don't expect perfection under pressure.

- A Word of Advice:
  Add extra excitement at the beginning of the trail, telling children that the treasure at the end will be shared out to favour the team which finds it first... but be warned, mistakes often happen when hunters are competing, so keep the clues simple and remind them...

> **SOLVE EACH CLUE CAREFULLY - DON'T JUMP THE GUN!**

USING PARALLEL TRAILS

Parallel trails can be great fun for two or more teams. Keep them moving separately or bring them together at points. PERSONALISE your own trails. Place a letter on a red, or blue card at each location which players write down as they follow the trail. Here are two short PARALLEL trails around school grounds.

CLUES FOR THE RED TEAM

CLUE 1:
Brave Oscar the Terrible likes eating bats and newt's kneebones.
take the first letter of each word to find your next letter
(= bottle bank)

CLUE 2:
(PICTURE CLUE)
GREEN HOUSE WINDOW
find this place to get your next letter

CLUE 3:
wave your arms F R O . about to attract D O . the team who have GO TO . the other part TO FIND N. of this clue
(= front door)

CLUE 4:
symbols to go on front door:
™! @ ú $ % #
use this code to find next letter
$=b !=e #=x ™=n ú=t %=o @=s
(= nest box)

CLUE 5:
Mark's motored bicycle, mentioned in Mean Machine Magazine, stands majestically most mornings masking Mr. Mann's motorcar.
cross out words beginning with m
(= in bicycle stands)

LAST CLUE:
You now have five letters. Arrange them to spell a vegetable. Return to base with your answer, and five leaves from plants you can name, to get your prize.
(e.g. beans)

Write, or photocopy clues onto different coloured paper for each team.
Give players a booklet of clues at onset of play, handing out alternative coloured
booklets to each group of players. Explain the game's format and OFF THEY GO.

CLUES FOR THE BLUE TEAM

CLUE 1:
Mark's motored bicycle,
mentioned in Mean Machine
Magazine, stands
majestically most mornings
masking Mr. Mann's motorcar.
*cross out words
beginning with m*
(= in bicycle stands)

CLUE 2:
(PICTORIAL CLUE)
B +
WHEEL   ARROW
*find this to find your
next letter*
(= wheelbarrow)

CLUE 3:
*attract the attention .
of the team that has .
NT the other part of .
OR this clue by waving .
THIS PLACE your arms
about madly * . EXT CLUE.
(= front door)

CLUE 4:
symbols to go on front door:
TM ! @ ú $ % #
use this code to find next letter
$=p !=a #=t TM=s ú=d %=i @=n
(= sand pit)

CLUE 5:
Brave Oscar the Terrible
likes eating bats and
newt's knee bones.
*take first letter of each
word to find your next letter*
(= bottle bank)

LAST CLUE:
*You now have five letters.
Arrange them to spell an animal.
Return to base with your
answer, and five leaves
from plants you can name,
to get your prize. *
(e g. horse)

FAMILY TREASURE HUNTS

Family gatherings bring together different ages and skills.

Plan a treasure hunting trail that takes into account INDIVIDUAL ABILITIES AND INTERESTS, encouraging social skills to develop within teams.

Set up two teams consisting of different ages, to compete for fun. This calls for mixed types of clue, each labelled for an individual's attention. After 30 seconds, the player can call upon others in the team to help if needs be.

DIFFERENT AGES can work side-by-side, or compete. Clues specialised to attract an adult's love of roses, or a child's knowledge of modern fairy tales, will help to hook your hunters into the game. Personalising clues lets teenagers show off their knowledge of pop music alongside toddlers asked to identify pictures, or an adult's geographical or historical expertise.

1st letter of answer

She sang "We'll meet again..." __

pic of a dinosaur __

They recorded "Zooropa" __

(= V D U)

- Store used clues for later inspiration. Prepare new clues in quiet moments for future games and swap clues with friends.

Family treasure hunts are ideal entertainment wherever you are. Gatherings in unfamiliar places bring unusual articles into play.

- Bear in mind what your players know. Will they be aware of where the clothes pegs are kept? Will they know of the sofa in the spare room upstairs? If there may be a choice of location for some clues, remind players when the game begins…although try not to choose the most unusual option as excited hunters are likely to overlook this alternative.

- And what about some odd information to tax them?

Does a full-grown blue whale weigh:
130 centimetres?
60 grams?
130 tons?

match the right answer with the place that hides your next clue

130 centimetres = bath mat
60 grams = north pole
130 tons = front door

- Making clues FOR EACH OTHER is an educational task children enjoy mastering. An appreciation of others' abilities, and practical attention to an orderly planning system, are experienced in this task. Mental and physical activity is attractive to both adults and children alike. When the children can set trails for each other, and yourselves, you know that your efforts have not been in vain!

Whatever their age, wherever the place, treasure hunts are GOOD CLEAN FUN.

GENERAL KNOWLEDGE CLUES

These are a brilliant way of boosting children's educational wisdom and encourage CONSULTATION between the ages.

Within the families, some players may be less mobile than others. Collective trails divide different tasks among different players according to their skills.

WRITE CLUES TO SUIT YOUR HUNTERS' ABILITIES

- When there may be doubt about an answer, give them a choice of answers:

  Q: If I have a dozen eggs, how many do I have?
  6 = microwave 12 = toothbrush
  13 = on fridge

- Creating a whole trail in this style is simplicity itself and, by flicking through an encyclopaedia to get ideas, you'll be surprised how much YOU can learn! If necessary, give some ridiculous choices of answer to steer them towards the right one.

1st letter of answer

the pied flycatcher lays pale ____ eggs __

Golden Delicious and Granny Smiths are types of____

opposite of hot __

marsupial amicably known as Skippy __

twelfth month of the year __

eight-legged sea creature __

opposite of shut __

eighteenth letter of alphabet __

(= back door)

General knowledge clues can be slipped craftily into clues to give your hunters a chance to boast their knowledge. Team games allows ignorant ears to glean information from other players, but keep clues FUN and EASY, not BORING.

1st letter of answer

The capital city of England ___

Five plus three ___

The letter after F in the alphabet ___

Eight-legged sea creature ___

(= lego)

- You can use school work, either as challenges (a short maths test with every correct sum scoring extra bounty points), or include the tasks in your clues:

a) 4 + 2 =   b) 7 + 1 =
c) 3 + 2 =   d) 1 + 6 =

* Use your answers to spell out the place where your next clue hides *

8 = v   6 = o   7 = n   5 = e

___ ___ ___ ___

(= oven)

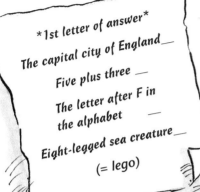

- 'Historical' anecdotes can hide useful information.

a hUNDred million yEaRs ago, britAin disapPeared for a long tIme under a

shaLLOW sea full of sea creatures.

(capitals in red)

write down red letters to find where your next clue hides

___ ___ ___ ___ ___ ___ ___

(= under a pillow)

- School projects can be included in clues, too. Foreign languages, a hobby, anything of special interest to a particular child.

> **ENTERTAINMENT IS DEVELOPED THROUGH WIDE USE OF SKILLS**

Educational elements in treasure hunting games are included as you, the games master, choose. Use what you want, deliver it how you will and play towards your hunters' need for mental stimulation as a source of FUN.

HUNTING AROUND ONE ROOM

Treasure hunting WITHIN ONE ROOM can be as easy or complicated as your hunters can manage.

- Simple hunts need no clues. Liberally distribute pieces of bounty around the room, some bits hidden more carefully than others.

- To encourage early reading, or the learning of a foreign language, give WORDS to players who must match them up with PICTURES which are sprinkled around the room. Complete the task to receive a prize.

- Instead of written clues, SOUND can be used to direct hunters towards their prize. A well-known game is the 'HOT and COLD' instructional yells that indicate to a hunter how close, or far, they are from hidden TREASURE. Singing notes is another version of this game; the higher the pitch, the nearer their prize.

- Draw a telephone then find YOUR number in the telephone directory. (The next clue is tucked in the page of the directory where the clue-solver's own telephone number is located)

- DIFFERENT ROOMS allow for different types of trail. The kitchen may involve finding nutmeg, a room of books opens up author and subject knowledge, a bedroom holds the opportunity of tasks of tidying up as the game proceeds!

- Highlighting UNFAMILIAR OBJECTS ensures the hunt is full of surprises, and encourages your player's OBSERVATIONAL skills. Design your trail around festive decorations or souvenirs, with lettered attachments carefully placed to avoid breakages.

GREETINGS CARD TRAIL

Creating a trail around celebrational greeting cards is EASY and FUN, too. Put a word on the back of individual cards. Players have a booklet of clues to uncover each word in turn, leading them to the treasure.

CLUE 1:
IT ON CATS BABY TWO HAS
THAT CARD A FOR LOOK
*read this sentence
backwards*
(card with two kittens)

CLUE 2:
PARENTS ARE NOT SO YOUNG
*take first letter of each word to
find what to look for next*
(card with pansy)

CLUE 3:
love from Ian and Julie,
Heather and Tom.
*find this card and
your next word*

CLUE 4:
look for a card whose
picture has been drawn by
*IMAGERY ILLUSTRATIONS

CLUE 5:
1st letter of answer
How old is Clare? —
(7)
The DAY of her birthday? —
(wednesday)
3rd letter of her name?
Is it snowing?
(card with swan on it)

CLUE 6:
To find the sixth and last word,
look inside the card from JOY.
(write the word wastebin
INSIDE the card)
(the six words collected
could be: your, treasure,
hides, in, the, wastebin)

PLAN YOUR TRAIL

Setting a treasure hunting game is easy once you've planned the trail. Beware of SAFETY HAZARDS; avoid choosing locations with too many alternatives; and keep the action level HIGH.

- The first clue may need your assistance as players familiarise themselves with the format of play. Once solved, you will want them to scurry away and proceed unaided, so chose your first location well away from the starting base.

- Choose items that are DISTINCTIVE and easy to identify by your players. Once a clue is solved, the game springs into action and should not be frustrated by moving furniture, or peering for ages into a dark cupboard.

- As you write each clue, write its location on the back. This helps you lay the trail. Make a separate note of where the last clue will lead them, or where the treasure is to be hidden. When you are ready, set the trail then call your players together, instruct them, and let the HUNT begin.

- PROMINENT clues can be written on scrolls or on torn scraps that fit together to build a treasure map as the game proceeds. Access to a computer allows for minuscule lettering that requires a hand-held magnifying glass. Cut-out newspaper print is similarly effective, too.

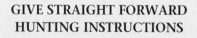

| GIVE STRAIGHT FORWARD HUNTING INSTRUCTIONS |

- Tell them FRONT DOOR MAT rather than just the word MAT.

- As you plan your trail KEEP YOUR HUNTERS IN MIND. Will they know where the honey is kept? Or Aunty's telephone directory?

- TEAMS should be kept apart to keep unwanted interaction at bay. Plan your trail to travel upstairs then downstairs, in one room, then another.

ADVANCE PREPARATION

You can place a clue anywhere from under the telephone to inside grandma's coat pocket. Smuggling a clue onto one of the players before the game begins adds extra SURPRISE.

- An unusual location, like the inside of a vacuum cleaner, extends the children's knowledge of such things.

- For the less mobile, 'the cushion behind you' and 'inside your pen' are just two suggestions for locations made possible through secret planning beforehand.

- TEAMS of players need SPACE to find clues. Plan your locations to allow for an excited scrambling for clues…and remind all players to THINK if there could be an alternative location, before they wreck the place!

- Treasure hunting games are beneficial to the trail-setters too. Not only can you relax whilst the hunt is in progress, but the challenges along the way can be useful too! "Put these building bricks back in their bag before proceeding," or, "Find a home for these pairs of clean socks. In one of the drawers your next clue hides."

- Creating a hunt around small, transportable objects is useful when visiting unfamiliar homes. Choose objects such as a hairbrush, packet of seeds, an apple etc. and write your clues. When you are ready to play, distribute the objects around a room and present the clues. As each is solved, the players note down the letter attached to each object, to build up their prize-winning word.

Convalescing children, unable to stand the pace of a race, can be enjoyably entertained in this way, and the game can be played almost anywhere.

A TOUCH OF HUMOUR

Kids love humour - jokes, riddles, tongue twisters, mischievous language and ridiculous words and rhyme.

- Use familiar jokes to solve clues:

WHA* IS GRE*N AND HAIRY *ND GOE* U* AND DOWN?

Answer: A G**SEBERRY I* A LIFT.

* fill in the missing letters to find your next clue *

(= teaspoon)

- ENTERTAINING riddles can be found in verse books, on joke pages or create your own. Scan the lines to uncover hidden words, saving those you can't use now for a later date.

- Amusing general knowledge questions prove useful, too.

What are the seeds of an oak tree called? Henry? peanuts? acorns ?

match your answer with the words below to find your next clue

Henry = radio peanuts = bath mat acorns = settee

- SURPRISE is a source of laughter and enjoyment for treasure trailers. Unusual locations for your clues; unusual (but readable) words within your clues, and unusual challenges along the way all keep your hunters smiling.

- Surprising your players with plastic spiders is fun for all but the weak hearted. Putting clues in strange places, such as in the jam pot, is good for a giggle too, but do protect your clue with clear sticky tape beforehand! One of the biggest surprises for small children is finding a clue in one of their pockets, which you planted in there before the game began.

Humour is self-generating when teams are actively encouraged to INTERACT.

- Written clues that HIDE solutions inside them can be fashioned to appeal to a child's sense of silliness.

Dear Oscar,

Graham is very sad. Crispin, his pet worm, died yesterday.

On a brighter note, he now has a pet earwig called Lucy.

Lots of love from,
Aunty Rita. x x x x x

write down the CAPITAL letters to find your next clue

_ _ _ _ _ _ _

helP! i am a tyrannosaurus rex wIth a toothache. pleAse send me a deNtist fOr my tea, i mean, to See my Tooth.

lOve frOm

growLer.

(put capitals in green)

* write down the letters written in green bat's blood to find your next clue *

_ _ _ _ _ _ _ _

(= piano stool)

- Another use of humorous writing is to include words or letters of different styles.

ROBIN HOOD'S TEAM

clue 4:

Will Friar Tuck please stop picking his nose!

*write down....
5th letter: ___   7th letter: ___
18th letter: ___   31st letter: ___
...to find your next clue*

(= fish)

- A theme to your game can lend scope for silly humour, as well as some serious impersonations. Surprise your players with unusual clues.

WHAT ABOUT THE TREASURE

Treasure at the end of your trail can be sugary, playful or fruity depending on your players and what is to hand. Children can MAKE THEIR OWN treasure to compete for along the trail. Painted coins cut from gold card are ideal. Then, the players with most treasure coins at the end of the game become the victors; they are entitled to propose a forfeit for the losers.

- Golden foil wrapped chocolate coins are ideal. (Look out for post-Christmas sales.) Golden toffee, fudge or honeycombed nuggets are equally unsuitable for the teeth!

- For COMPETITIVE TEAM GAMES, treasure should be sharable between players, the winning team receiving first choice or the biggest cut of bounty on offer.

- For INDIVIDUALS, choose a suitably wrapped gift - a small toy or a new bar of luxury soap. Inexpensive prizes are vital to avoid setting a costly precedent for future games.

- Treasure can be hidden along the trail or awarded for challenges performed on the way.

Singing a song, drawing a picture or winning a quick quiz result in bonus bounty - you judge how much bounty, depending on the skill used.

Games with a THEME allow unusual treasure to appear at the end of the trail. Royalty welcome jelly-jewelled sweets or diamond-dusted emerald grapes on a silver platter. Pirates are greedy for loot, strings of beads and toy parrots. Private Eyes enjoy certificates of glory, slices of chocolate cake or their very own magnifying glasses.

- Sometimes a CHOICE of prize brings an added twist to the end of the trail. Here, each player selects a folded note which discloses what they will win. Add a booby prize like a cabbage, or something unexpected like a coloured candle.

INSTRUCTIONS FOR HUNTERS

Each treasure hunting game can be different with different rules of play. You, as games master, are in charge of informing the players what to expect and how to observe the decorum of play. Before the game begins, explain the format of your clues and what type of game it is to be...competitive or team play, personalised clues or a random 'free for all'.

Show your players an extra clue you have made, pointing out which words are INSTRUCTIONS and which words are there for them to use when solving clues.

When players have to collect letters on the way, or save their clues to construct a treasure map, TELL THEM BEFOREHAND! Players must know before they begin, if they are competing against another team, for treasure, or if there is no competitive element at all.

Provide your players with the necessary equipment - a pen each and scrap paper, and a container or bag to hold the clues or treasure they collect along the way. Other implements (such as a magnifying glass) might be necessary to undertake the hunt you have devised, so be sure to equip your players accordingly.

It is necessary to make clear which areas of the house or garden are OUT OF BOUNDS. You can reinforce this with No Entry signs for younger players.

And remind children...

> **CLUES CRACKED, NOT HEADS,**
> **SHOW THE WAY TO TREASURE**

FUND RAISING FUN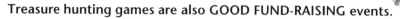

Treasure hunting games are also GOOD FUND-RAISING events.

Draw an exciting map on a large sheet of card thick enough to hold map pins. On the back of the card mark a cross (this is where the treasure lies). Cut some small paper squares and number them. Arm yourself with a notebook, pen and map pins, and a notice of play:

PINPOINT LONG-JOHN'S HOARD OF HIDDEN TREASURE TO WIN YOURSELF A SHARE OF HIS BOUNTY.

Display a jar of mixed sweets, an assortment of bath-time delights or perhaps a selection of crystallised fruits as your prize, and invite your players to pin numbered squares onto your map. Note the entrant's name, address or telephone number alongside their number in your notebook and at the end of the day's play, reveal the winning pin, or the pin closest to the treasure.

Alternatively, provide a trail of clues presented in a booklet, that leads hunters around the grounds of your fund-raising event. Players need to be given a pencil then to collect the letters or words which you have securely attached at each clue's location. Keep prizes cheap and cheerful to ensure the profitability of your game.

One BEAUTY of this game is that clue booklets can present clues in a random order...this prevents following trailers earwigging their way through the game.

> On the remaining pages you will find several sets of clues to get you going. Some are linked as specialist trails. Others are random examples for you to dip into if your mind remains blank. They give ideas for clue locations and can be adapted to suit the age and ability of YOUR players.

ONE ROOM TREASURE HUNT - A GAME TO TRY

A TRANSPORTABLE treasure hunt, playable IN ONE ROOM, is very useful to have pre-prepared. Choose your objects then conceal a letter on each one.
The players, with a booklet of clues, collect their letters to spell a word.

CLUE 1:
AFTER HER
3 1 4 2 8   5 6 7
use these numbered letters to find your next clue

___ ___ ___ ___ ___ ___ ___
1   2   3   4   5   6   7

(= feather)

CLUE 2:
(PICTORIAL CLUE)
_ _ _ _
(= note pad)

CLUE 3:
HANDLE COLDER
swap the H and the C
(= candle holder)

CLUE 4
ESAC LICNEP
* write backwards *
_ _ _ _ _ _
(= pencil case)

CLUE 5:
WITCHES ARE TRICKING CUTE HAMSTERS
take first letter of each word to find your next clue
_ _ _ _ _
(= watch)

CLUE 6:
You should now have five letters that spell out a word. Whisper this word to the games master to get your prize.

For this game, the five objects used are: a feather, a note pad, a candle holder, pencil case and a watch.

> **FOR MORE THAN ONE PLAYER, PUT CLUES IN A DIFFERENT ORDER**

READY-MADE FAMILY FUN

Here are some FAMILY treasure hunting clues to give you some inspiration.
Write each clue then write on the back where it needs to be placed before
the start of play. Label each clue with the player's name.

CLUE 1: (everyone)
1st letter of answer
Popeye's wife __
Planet and ocean king __
Ms Bergman's Christian name __
15th letter of alphabet __
Peter Pan's home __
(= onion)

CLUE 2: (8 year old)
shrew lay under big log
* take middle letter of each word to
find your next clue *

_ _ _ _ _
(= radio)

CLUE 3: (everyone)
_ _ _ _ _ _ Dracula.
_ _ _ _ _ blind mice.
" _ _ _ _ _ way to heaven."
Be__t wishes _ _ _ _ _, Lucy.
I'm on _ _ _ of the world.
fill in spaces
(= 3rd stair from top)

CLUE 4: (6 year old)
Humming and groaning,
Spinning and foaming.
I am the machine
That gets trousers clean.
(= washing machine)

CLUE 5: (4 year old)
(PICTORIAL CLUE of teddy)
look inside his sock

CLUE 6: (7 year old)
on elephant of picture with mug
read backwards

CLUE 7: (3 year old)
PICTURE CLUE of game or toy whose
picture has been cut out of catalogue)
the next clue hides here

CLUE 8: (6 year old)
D E D D E R   D O T
*change every D for a P to
find your next clue*

_ _ _ _ _ _ _ _
(= pepper pot)

CLUE 9: (7 year old)
Mime a nursery rhyme to the other players.
If they guess it correctly, the games master
will give you your next clue. If not, try again.

CLUE 10: (adult)
E A T   H O T   P O T S
10 7 4 5 3 1 6 2 9 8
put these letters in order

_ _ _ _ _ _ _ _ _ _
1 2 3 4 5 6 7 8 9 10
(= toothpaste)

CLUE 11: (14 year old)
R E D   F I G
*rearrange these letters to find
where your next clue lies*

_ _ _ _ _ _
(= fridge)

CLUE 12: (10 year old)
1st letter of answer
Planet with rings of dust __
Tenth month of year __
Robin Crusoe's companion __
First man in Eden __
(= sofa)

When the last clue has been hidden, place suitable treasure at the location
the last clue leads the players to.

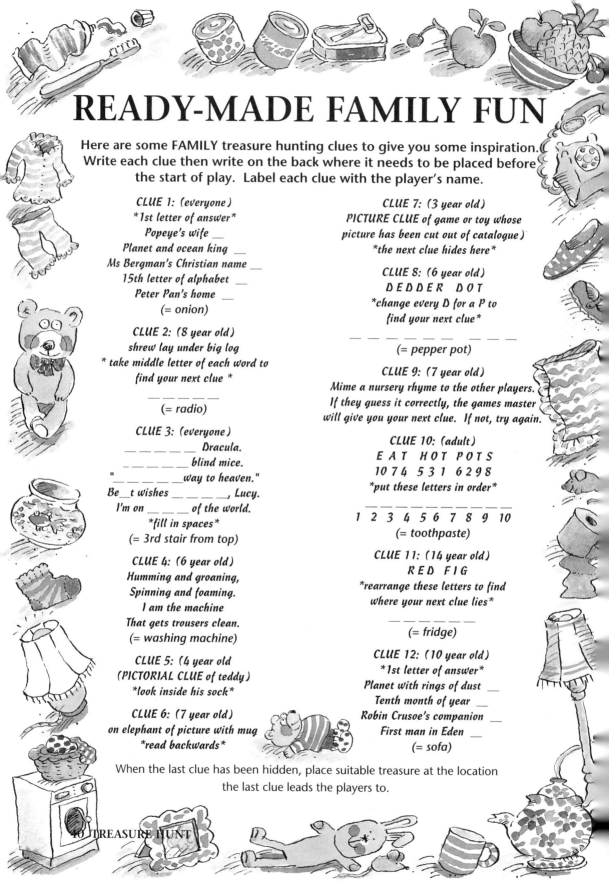

FUNNY CLUES

Put some clues in each of your trails that will make your players giggle. Get your players to behave strangely, or set them searching in odd locations for their clues.

Find a fruit that looks like green eyeballs. (= grapes)

TASTY VERRUCAS
* take first letter of each word *
__ __ (= TV)

Look through smelly socks to find your next clue.
(= inside sock in dirty clothes basket)

SLUG PIE
Take some of this lovely dinner to find your next clue.
5th letter, 2nd letter, 3rd letter, 4th letter: __ __ __ __
(= plug)

kNickers shOuld be kepT nICEly in your BottOm drAweR, Dear.
(put capitals in red)
write down red letters
__ __ __ __ __ __ __ __ __ __ __
(= notice board)

In the sink, sink, sink,
Where I drink, drink, drink,
Is a black, black hole,
And a pink, pink, roll.

(= rolled up pink paper in plug hole. Inside roll of paper put a small cut-out cardboard fly or spider-like fluff to surprise your players.)

ROASTED STOAT
1 2 3 4 5 6 7   4 5 2 3 5
use these numbered letters
_____
5 2 3 4 5 6 1
(= toaster)

(PICTURE CLUE) wellington boot
(put toy spider in boot)

TAM ROOD REDNU
write backwards
_____
(= under door mat)
(put creepy crawly under mat)

Jammed in a traffic jam,
I'm going potty, potty, pot.
write down the 3-lettered words from the sentence above
___ ___
(cover the clue in sticky tape and put it in the pot!)

COVERED IN JELLY BABIES
cross off first and last word
(make up jelly, add clue, allow to set before game begins...provide a spoon for each player!)

grunt like pigs to find the team with the other half SO of this clue.

act like kangaroos to find the team with the other half of this clue. FA

READY-MADE CLUES

FAIR CRUSH
*change the F for an H and the
C for a B to find your next clue*
(= hair brush)

ALL HERB MUSTARD
cross out the H
cross out the last 5 letters
write other letters backwards

_ _ _ _ _ _ _ _

(= umbrella)

(PICTURE CLUE)
SUN   WINE GLASSES

_ _ _   _ _ _ _ _ _

(= sunglasses)

HUGE ANTS NIBBLE DOWN
BIG APPLE GROVES
*take first letter of each word
to find your next clue*

_ _ _ _ _   _ _ _

(= handbag)

Terrible stOrms wReCk wHale's
birthday party (capitals in red)
*write down red letters to
find your next clue *

_ _ _ _ _

(= (octopus?))

TOOB   NOTGNILLEW
*write backwards to find where
your next clue hides*
(= wellington boots)

1st letter of answer
9th month of the year __
21st letter of alphabet __
grandma's husband __
opposite of awake __
they pull Santa's sleigh __
(= sugar)

Last letter of answer
opposite to the antarctic __
a feather pen __
letter before P in alphabet __
opposite to the arctic __
white drink we get from cows __
(= clock)

How many letters in the alphabet?
32 = tennis racket
26 = jam pot
25 = telephone

What is the tenth month?
February = toaster
November = television
October = settee

Baby eaRwigs wEar smAll reD
Kneepads wheN learnIng to
skateboard For plEasure.
(capitals in red)

*write down red letters to
find next clue*

_ _ _ _ _ _ _ _ _

(= breadknife)

cAtch a Fat SealiOn
(capitals in red)
*unscramble the red letters
to find your next clue*

_ _ _ _ _

(= sofa)

rabbits only leave lettuce if
nice green parsley is nearby
*take first letter of the
words above to find where
your next clue hides*

_ _ _ _ _ _ _   _ _ _
(= rolling pin)

FAT CLAP
• swop over the first letters of each word
_AT _LAP
(= cat flap)

IRON, GOLD OR SILVER,
WHICH OF THEM WILL DO ?
WHEN I WANT TO FLATTEN CLOTHES
AND MAKE THEM SMOOTH FOR YOU.
(= iron)

KCOLC MRALA
• write these words backwards

_ _ _ _ _ _ _ _ _ _
(= alarm clock)

TO WASTE TIME, THROW PAPER
TOWARDS THE TOY BASKET
• cross out words beginning with T
(= waste paper basket)

I MAKE BREAD TURN BROWN
AND HOT,
DROP SLICES DOWN INTO MY SLOT.
(=toaster)

STAND UP BROTHER
◗ I £ ○ ☆ % ✳ ▼ • ✪ I ⇨ ♥ ✖
• use these coded letters to make
four new words

☆ % ◗ I   ✳ £ ○
_ _ _ _   _ _ _

£ ○ ☆   ▼ • % ◗ I ⇨
_ _ _   _ _ _ _ _ _
(= dust pan and brush)

PUPPLE PATH POTTLE
• change every P for a B to find
where your next clue hides
(= bubble bath bottle)

IN M.T. MILK BOTTLE
• read this clue aloud to hear
where your next clue hides
(= in empty milk bottle)

FIND A ROTTING PIN
• change every T to an L before
looking for your next clue
(= rolling pin)

BASKET INSIDE DIRTY CLOTHES
4   1   2   3
• put words in order to find
where your next clue hides
(= inside dirty clothes basket)

OUR PURRRRRFECT
PET EATS HERE.
(= cat bowl)

A house for dolls
Is small inside.
A clue by the cooker
Is trying to hide.
(= dolls house cooker)

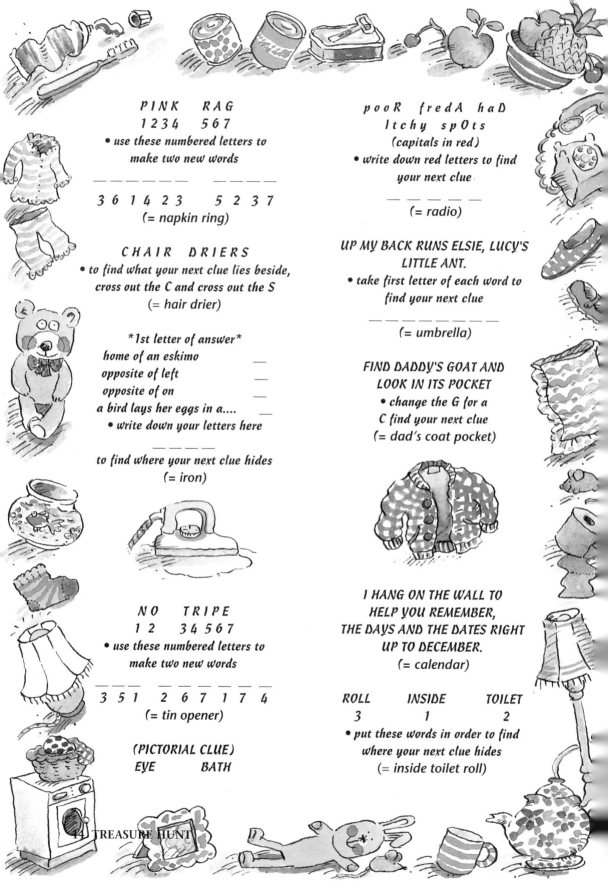

PINK   RAG
1234   567
- use these numbered letters to
make two new words

___ ___ ___ ___   ___ ___ ___
3 6 1 4 2 3   5 2 3 7
(= napkin ring)

CHAIR   DRIERS
- to find what your next clue lies beside,
cross out the C and cross out the S
(= hair drier)

1st letter of answer
home of an eskimo   ___
opposite of left   ___
opposite of on   ___
a bird lays her eggs in a.... ___
- write down your letters here

___ ___ ___ ___
to find where your next clue hides
(= iron)

NO   TRIPE
1 2   34 567
- use these numbered letters to
make two new words

___ ___ ___ ___ ___ ___ ___ ___
3 5 1   2 6 7 1 7 4
(= tin opener)

(PICTORIAL CLUE)
EYE   BATH

pooR fredA haD
Itchy spOts
(capitals in red)
- write down red letters to find
your next clue

___ ___ ___ ___ ___
(= radio)

UP MY BACK RUNS ELSIE, LUCY'S
LITTLE ANT.
- take first letter of each word to
find your next clue

___ ___ ___ ___ ___ ___ ___ ___
(= umbrella)

FIND DADDY'S GOAT AND
LOOK IN ITS POCKET
- change the G for a
C find your next clue
(= dad's coat pocket)

I HANG ON THE WALL TO
HELP YOU REMEMBER,
THE DAYS AND THE DATES RIGHT
UP TO DECEMBER.
(= calendar)

ROLL   INSIDE   TOILET
3   1   2
- put these words in order to find
where your next clue hides
(= inside toilet roll)

FLAN   CASE
✪ ➡ ▲ ✳   ◯ ▲ ☆ ♥
• use the code above to crack this clue

✪ ▲ ◯ ♥
___ ___ ___ ___

✪ ➡ ▲ ✳ ✳ ♥ ➡
___ ___ ___ ___ ___ ___ ___
(= face flannel)

**MOTHER'S FLIPPERS
TOUCH HER TOES**
• change the F to an S to
find your next clue
(= mum's slippers)

OLD   PAINTS
1 2 3   4 5 6 7 8 9
• use these numbered letters
to find your next clue

___ ___ ___ ___ ___ ___ ___ ___ ___ ___
4 6 5 7 1 9 8 1 1 2
(= piano stool)

a MIRROR IN the flower BED
Reflects the blOOMs
(capitals in red)
• write down red letters to
find your next clue

___ ___ ___ ___ ___ ___ ___ ___
___ ___ ___ ___ ___ ___
(= mirror in bedroom)

DRESS MUMMY'S INSIDE NIGHT
4   2   1   3
• put these words in order
to find your next clue
(= inside mummy's nightdress)

(PICTORIAL CLUE)
NUT   XMAS CRACKER

FUR, HAIR OR SCALES,
WHICH OF THESE WILL DO ?
IF I WANT TO WEIGH OUT FLOUR
AND MAKE A CAKE FOR YOU.
(= kitchen scales)

___ ___ ___ ___ AND PEPPER
___ ___ ___ ___ AND
VINEGAR CRISPS.
• one word will fit into both spaces -
what is that word?
(= salt)

A CLUE 4 U, IS IN A POT 4 T.
• read this clue aloud to hear where
your next clue hides
(= tea pot)

POOR   KNICKERS!
• change the P for a D,
change the I for an
O and remove the S to
find your next clue
(= door knocker)

• **1ST LETTER OF ANSWER**
an animal that has kittens __
the nut of an oak tree __
Maid Marian's hero __
colour of blood __
colour of carrots __
day after Monday __
(= carrot)

S O R E   E L E P H A N T
10 7 11 9   4 3 2 5 6 12 8 1
• put some of these numbered letters
into order to find your next clue

— — — — — — — — —
1 2 3 4 5 6 7 8 9
(= telephone)

**EVERY GOOD GIRL
CLEARS UP PROPERLY**
• take first letter of each word

— — — — — — —
(= egg cup)

(PICTURE CLUE)
DOG   SHIRT
(= collar)

F R E E   H E R !
• change the H into a Z and
make one word

— — — — — — —
(= freezer)

sLuNg HaIrY bOoT wEIl
(capitals in red)
• cross out red letters and write
down the letters that are left

— — — — — — — — —
(= sugar bowl)

A
E   R
G   G
E   A
M
• starting with the right-hand G, read
this clue in a clockwise direction
(= game gear)

W __ S T __   P __ P __ R
1   2   1   2

B __ S K __ T
1   2
• put an A into spaces numbered 1,
put an E into spaces numbered 2.
(= waste paper basket)

LOOK BEHIND THE SET TEA
• read clue aloud to hear where
your next clue hides
(= behind settee)

FIND A ROCK THAT GOES TICK TOCK
• change the R into a CL to
find where your next clue hides
(= ticking clock)

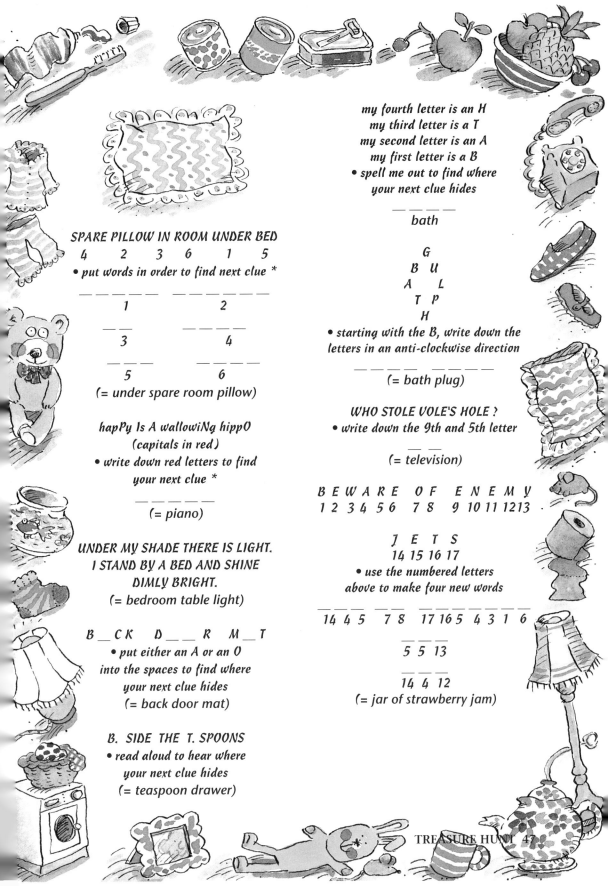

my fourth letter is an H
my third letter is a T
my second letter is an A
my first letter is a B
• spell me out to find where
your next clue hides

— — — —
bath

SPARE PILLOW IN ROOM UNDER BED
4   2   3   6   1   5
• put words in order to find next clue *

— — —   — —
   1   2

— — —   — —
   3   4

— — —   — —
   5   6
(= under spare room pillow)

hapPy Is A wallowiNg hippO
(capitals in red)
• write down red letters to find
your next clue *

— — — — —
(= piano)

UNDER MY SHADE THERE IS LIGHT.
I STAND BY A BED AND SHINE
DIMLY BRIGHT.
(= bedroom table light)

B _ C K   D _ _ _   R M _ T
• put either an A or an O
into the spaces to find where
your next clue hides
(= back door mat)

B. SIDE THE T. SPOONS
• read aloud to hear where
your next clue hides
(= teaspoon drawer)

G
B   U
A   L
T   P
H
• starting with the B, write down the
letters in an anti-clockwise direction

— — — —   — — — —
(= bath plug)

WHO STOLE VOLE'S HOLE ?
• write down the 9th and 5th letter

— —
(= television)

B E W A R E   O F   E N E M Y
1 2 3 4 5 6   7 8   9 10 11 1213

J E T S
14 15 16 17
• use the numbered letters
above to make four new words

— — — — — — — — — — — —
14 4 5   7 8   17 16 5   4 3 1 6

— — —
5 5 13

— — —
14 4 12
(= jar of strawberry jam)

• 1st letter of answer
three add three = __
one add one = __
three take away two = __
month after September = __
capital city of England = __
(= stool)

DADDY'S LOCKS OF
BROWN AND GREY,
REST IN HERE WHEN PUT AWAY.
• change the L to a S to find
where your next clue hides
(= dad's sock drawer)

T O Y   B R A I N
• change the B into a T to find
where your next clue lies
(= train set)

G O L D E N   V E S T
✳ I □ ▲ ☆ ○   ▼ ☆ ⇨ ★
• use the code above to
make two new words

__ __ __ __   __ __ __ __ __
I ▼ ☆ ○   ✳ □ I ▼ ☆
(= oven glove)

OUR ROUGH, ROUGH, ROUGH,
PET SLEEPS HERE.
• read this clue aloud to find
your next clue.
(= dog basket)

CALL ME AND I'LL RING,
DISTANT VOICES,
CLOSE I'LL BRING.
DOCTOR SALT OR P.C. BRINE,
WHEN YOU DIAL UP 999.
(= telephone)

F E E T B A L L   B E E T S
• change every E to an
O to find next clue
(= football boots)

FIND SANDBAG UNDER TABLE
• change the S into an H before
you look for your next clue
(= handbag under table)

A
E   T
T   O
L   W
E
• starting with the T
on the left, write down
the letters in a clockwise direction

___ ___ ___   ___ ___ ___ ___ ___

(= tea towel)